ARCHBISHOP'S WELCOME

Welcome, dear visitor, to Westminster Cathedral.

This great church has a very special place in the recent history of the Catholic Church in our country and, by its very presence at the heart of the City of London, it proclaims far and wide something of Catholic belief and worship.

I know you will be inspired by the beauty and scale of the building, which is a testimony to the vision of my predecessor, Cardinal Henry Vaughan, and his architect, John Francis Bentley.

Above all, I hope that you will experience something of the invitation to prayer which permeates this building, and that you will quietly be able to be at peace with God and yourself within its portals.

May God bless you during your visit to Westminster Cathedral and may His peace be in your heart as you visit this place, and remain with you as you journey on your way.

May God bless you.

+ *Cormac Card. Murphy-O'Connor*

H.E. Cardinal Cormac Murphy-O'Connor
Archbishop of Westminster

INTRODUCTION

Westminster Cathedral is the largest and most important Catholic church in England and Wales. Not only is it the seat of the Cardinal Archbishop of Westminster, it also represents a Catholic presence at the heart of our nation, and a visible link both with the religious history of our own nation and the Church throughout the world.

The origins of Westminster Cathedral arise from the long and traumatic history of the Roman Catholic Church in this country since the Reformation. After centuries of discrimination and persecution, Roman Catholics were given full rights as citizens in 1829. In the decades that followed, immigration (from Ireland, above all) swelled the numbers and confidence of the Roman Catholic community, so that when Pope Pius IX restored the Roman Catholic dioceses and bishops in 1850, it was ready to assume a prominent role in the life of this country.

Under two outstanding Archbishops of Westminster, Cardinal Nicholas Wiseman (1850–1865) and Cardinal Henry Edward Manning (1865–1892), the Roman Catholic Church assumed a key role in national life. Their successor, Cardinal Herbert Vaughan (1892–1903), desired to enshrine this achievement in permanent form.

A site had already been purchased in the rapidly developing area of Victoria, but Cardinal Manning had hesitated to expend on a cathedral money which should first be used for schools and relief of the poor. The energetic Cardinal Vaughan had no such qualms and proceeded with the construction of Westminster Cathedral – a project which caused some disquiet to the Establishment but which, concealed by the lofty mansion blocks of Victoria, could at least be tolerated.

Cardinal Vaughan's first preference was for a Gothic cathedral or a Roman-style basilica, but his chosen architect, John Francis Bentley, persuaded him to adopt the exotic Byzantine style, for three reasons. Firstly, there would be no possibility of comparison with the exquisite (and authentic) Gothic architecture of Westminster Abbey. Secondly, Byzantine churches, centred on domes rather than narrow arches, allow for a large, uncluttered space, most suitable to the Roman Catholic liturgy. Thirdly, because design in Byzantine churches is applied (rather than integral to the architecture), they can be built quickly and relatively inexpensively, while decoration is left to the resources of subsequent generations.

The foundation stone of the cathedral was laid on 29 June 1895 and, eight years later, the cathedral was open for worship. Sadly, the first major service that took place was the funeral of its founder, Cardinal Vaughan, on 26 June 1903. Bentley himself had died in the previous year.

Their achievement has been to create a living centre for the Catholic Church in this land. Westminster Cathedral is not only a religious shrine proclaiming the presence and character of the Catholic Church in our society; it is an architectural gem, a prominent landmark, and (thanks to its world-famous choir) one of the major artistic centres of the country.

TIMELINE

1651 Following the defeat of Charles II at Worcester, 4,000 Scottish prisoners are quartered in Tothill Fields by Oliver Cromwell.

1665 Tothill Fields used as a burial site during the Great Plague.

1834 The Middlesex County Prison is built on Tothill Fields.

1850 The Diocese of Westminster created at the Restoration of the Catholic Hierarchy by Pope Pius IX, with Nicholas Wiseman as first Archbishop.

1867 Initial purchase of site adjacent to present cathedral for £35,000.

1883 Middlesex County Prison demolished.

1884 Cardinal Manning buys the site of the Middlesex County Prison for £55,000, partly funded by the exchange of the 1867 purchase.

1894 Herbert Vaughan, the third Archbishop of Westminster, begins building, with John Francis Bentley as the chosen architect.

1895 The foundation stone is laid on 29 June.

1896 The foundations are completed and by 1903 the fabric of the building is in position.

1903 First regular celebration of daily Mass and Divine Office in the cathedral.

Edward Elgar conducts first London performance of John Henry Newman's *The Dream of Gerontius*.

1906 Unveiling and blessing of the *baldacchino* at Christmas Midnight Mass.

1908 Decoration of Holy Souls Chapel completed.

Eucharistic Congress – 7 cardinals, 130 bishops and 4,000 priests.

1910 Consecration of the cathedral.

1918 Eric Gill completes the Stations of the Cross.

1930 Body of St John Southworth is enshrined in Chapel of St George.

1935 Lady Chapel mosaics completed.

1955 Statue of Our Lady of Westminster placed in cathedral.

1958 Sculpture of St Thérèse of Liseux, by Giacomo Manzù.

1962 Mosaics in Blessed Sacrament Chapel, by Boris Anrep.

1975 Construction of piazza, opening view of cathedral on to Victoria Street.

1982 Visit of Pope John Paul II: first Papal Mass celebrated in Westminster Cathedral.

1995 Visit of HM the Queen during centenary celebrations. First visit of a sovereign to a Roman Catholic liturgy since the Reformation.

1999 Millennium Cross unveiled. Opening of the Jubilee Holy Door.

2005 Body of Cardinal Vaughan re-interred in Chapel of St Thomas.

Redevelopment of Victoria opens up new views of the cathedral.

ADMINISTRATORS OF WESTMINSTER CATHEDRAL

Mgr Patrick Fenton	1894–1904 (at Kensington)
Mgr John Moyes	1904–1905
Mgr Martin Howlett	1905–1947
Mgr Cuthbert Collingwood	1947–1954
Mgr Gordon Wheeler	1954–1964
Mgr George Tomlinson	1964–1967
Mgr Francis Bartlett	1967–1977
Mgr Oliver Kelly	1977–1989
Mgr Patrick O'Donoghue	1990–1993
Mgr George Stack	1993–2001
Mgr Mark Langham	2001–

THE NAVE

Standing in the centre of the cathedral, the first impression is of the immense space that unfolds before the visitor. Unlike the clustered columns and aisles of a Gothic cathedral, Byzantine domes allow for a vast central area, uncluttered by supports or pillars, so that up to two thousand people may have an uninterrupted view of the sanctuary as they worship. Note how the domes each rest upon four triangular 'pendentives' that rise out of the rectangular space below, a feature of the greatest Byzantine churches. From the cathedral in Pisa, John Francis Bentley borrowed the idea of concealing the internal buttresses with a gallery, running the entire length of the nave, bringing a grace and unity to this immense space. This is the highest (34 metres) and widest (18 metres) nave in the country. Clear Venetian glass windows flood the nave with light, representing to Byzantine understanding the Holy Spirit enlightening the Church.

The next impression is of bare brick, stained black by the soot of a century of candles and incense, and creating for many an atmosphere of mystery, yearning and poignancy. There are twelve and a half million bricks in the building, every one of them handmade. The task of decorating the walls of the cathedral has proceeded throughout the last hundred years. While the marble decoration of the nave's lower walls (symbolising the earth) is almost complete, it will be left to future ages to cover the vaults and domes in glittering mosaic (symbolic of the heavens).

Westminster Cathedral is dedicated to the Most Precious Blood of our Lord Jesus Christ, represented by the blood red columns of Norwegian granite near the main door. The visitor, entering between these columns, is reminded of the salvation won through the Precious Blood of Christ, poured out in his sacrifice on the Cross. The impressive green marble columns of the nave were carved from the same quarries as those used fifteen hundred years before in the great basilica of Haghia Sophia in

BELOW The statue of St Peter is a copy of the famous statue at St Peter's in Rome. Peter is represented holding keys, in memory of the promise of Christ: 'I will give you the keys of the kingdom of heaven' (Matthew 16:19).

BELOW The foot of the statue of St Peter is worn by the hands of countless pilgrims expressing their veneration of the saint and their communion with the See of Peter in Rome.

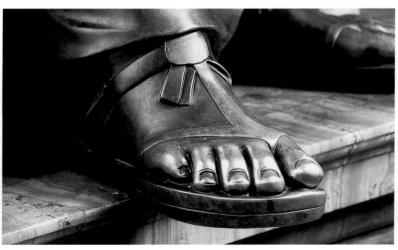

FAR LEFT Visitors light candles at the shrine of St Anthony. The cathedral is illuminated daily by hundreds of votive candles.
LEFT Almost sixty varieties of marble adorn the walls and floor of the cathedral.

Constantinople, whose design influenced Bentley above all other architecture. The exquisite capitals of the columns, in white Carrara marble, are carved after Byzantine originals; no two are the same, and yet their harmony is perfect – a testimony to the skill of the craftsmen who took three months, working in pairs, to carve each capital. The marble decoration of the cathedral is one of its glories; over fifty-seven different types of marble adorn the brickwork of the lower nave, including red *brèche sanguine* marble from Algeria, grey-green *cipollino* (whose markings imitate an onion skin) and blue *Azul Macauba* from Brazil. The red and green tones that pervade the nave are an unmistakable reference to the decoration of the great church of Constantinople.

The Stations of the Cross on the nave piers are carved in Hopton-Wood stone. They represent fourteen scenes, or 'stations', in the journey of Christ to his death, and are used for devotions during Lent. Each of the stations combines figures and words to convey the scene with great clarity and beauty. These are acknowledged to be the finest works of Eric Gill, the controversial sculptor and letterer. Engaged as a relatively unknown artist by Cardinal Bourne in 1913, the Westminster Stations sealed Gill's reputation, and are considered to be among the greatest artistic treasures of the cathedral. However, at the time of their installation, their radical style proved controversial: one parishioner ventured to comment that the stations did not look very nice, at which Gill snapped back that the subject was not very nice. A memorial inscription to Eric Gill, bearing his initials and dates, and the single word *lapidarius* (stonecutter) can be found at the foot of the fourteenth station.

The lighting pendants of the nave were installed in 1909, their design based on the descriptions of the oil-filled lamps that once

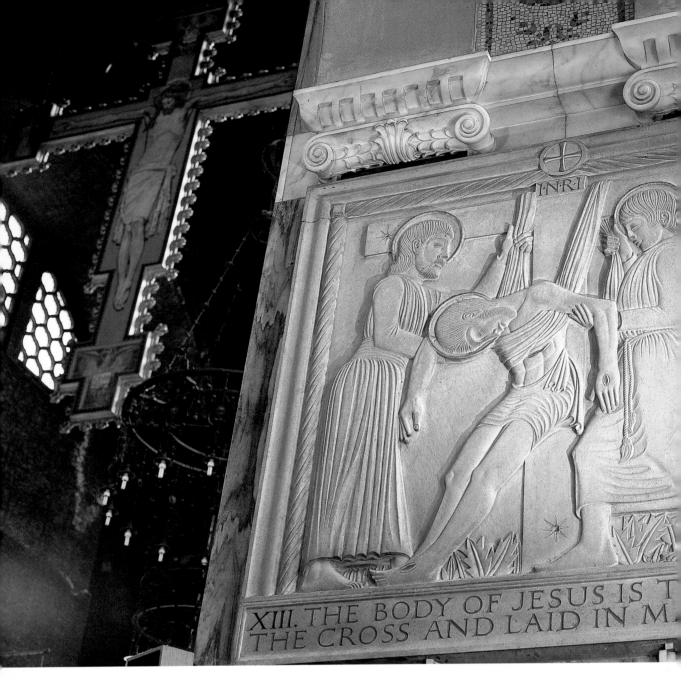

XIII. THE BODY OF JESUS IS T
THE CROSS AND LAID IN M

illuminated Haghia Sophia. The woodblock floor was originally intended to be covered with marble, representing fish swimming in the sea, but Bentley was constrained to abandon the idea for reasons of economy and warmth.

The original pulpit was enlarged in 1934 to celebrate Cardinal Francis Bourne's 30th anniversary as fourth Archbishop of Westminster. To commemorate the restoration of pilgrimage to Walsingham, an image in *opus sectile* of Our Lady of Walsingham was added. The twisted columns supporting the pulpit are decorated with Cosmati work, in imitation of the pulpits in medieval Italian cathedrals. The size of the pulpit reflects the considerable retinue that accompanied a cardinal at that time; now it is used only for major liturgical celebrations.

To the left of the entrance stands a fine statue of St Peter enthroned, proclaiming the communion of the Church in England and Wales with the See of Peter in Rome. It is a copy of the famed thirteenth-century statue in St Peter's Basilica, by Arnolfo di Cambio.

On the Feast of St Peter, the statue is adorned (like its Roman original) in papal tiara and vestments, and one foot bears the effects of a century of pilgrims' devotion. Beyond, on the wall of the aisle, are tablets recording the communion of the chief pastors of the Catholic Church in England and Wales with the Apostolic See of Rome.

Nearby is the entrance to the campanile, or bell tower. Soaring to 87 metres, it is topped by a cross containing a fragment of the True Cross, intended to bless the city that lies beneath it. The campanile is dedicated to St Edward the Confessor, patron of Westminster, and contains a single bell, the 'Great Edward', given by the Duchess of Norfolk in 1910. From the top of the campanile there are fine views of Westminster and the City.

The great rood (or crucifix) dominates the view of the nave ahead. Ten metres high and weighing two tonnes, it was carved in Belgium to John Francis Bentley's designs. Decorated by Christian Symons, the rood incorporates an elongated figure of Christ surrounded by the traditional symbols of the four evangelists and is a powerful architectural feature, uniting heaven to earth as it draws together the space of the nave. Its reverse bears the image of the Virgin of Sorrows, her heart pierced by a sword, accompanied by texts from the solemn Lenten hymn *Stabat Mater* especially chosen by Cardinal Vaughan. This is the image seen by the priest as he celebrates Mass: Mary, the representative of humanity, leading the congregation in worship of the divine mysteries, and transformed by the sacrifice of her Son.

ABOVE Our Lady of Walsingham, from the pulpit.
BELOW Light and shadow assume an architectural quality in Gill's stations.

BAPTISTRY

The chapels of Westminster Cathedral are deliberately arranged in order to depict the journey of the Christian from birth to death. That journey commences symbolically near the door of the cathedral in the baptistry, where children are born into a new life in Jesus Christ through the baptismal waters poured upon them.

The large octagonal font, 1.6 metres in diameter, was designed in 1901 by Francis Bentley, who was inspired by those to be found in early Christian basilicas. In those early days of the Church, baptism took place by total immersion in the font. That was never the intention at Westminster, where a smaller basin of white marble just inside the font is used more conveniently for baptisms. During the Easter Vigil, the climax of the Christian year, the baptismal waters are blessed here by the Archbishop. The gilded paschal candlestick with the Easter candle used on that occasion is usually kept near the font.

The marble covering the walls was paid for by the daughters of Francis Bentley. In the corner stands a statue of St John the Baptist, made of Cornish tin, a copy of the work by the celebrated Danish sculptor, Bertal Thorvaldsen, on the portico of the cathedral in Copenhagen.

On the wall just outside the baptistry can be found a small wooden statue of St Christopher, a poignant offering from the famous author, Hilaire Belloc, for the protection of his son and all the troops embarking for the First World War.

OPPOSITE PAGE A fine marble and gilt-bronze screen encloses the baptistry.
BELOW LEFT The statue of John the Baptist.
BELOW RIGHT The font, designed by Bentley, was carved in Rome.

CHAPEL OF ST GREGORY AND ST AUGUSTINE

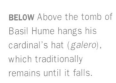

This chapel is dedicated to the saints who first brought the Gospel to England. Above the altar, Pope St Gregory sends St Augustine and his companions to these shores. Higher up, St Augustine is received by the pagan Ethelbert, King of Kent; Augustine was later to become the first Archbishop of Canterbury.

On the ceiling are portrayed early saints of England: St Wilfrid, St Benedict Biscop, St Cuthbert, St Edmund, St Bede the Venerable and St Osmund.

A panel in the arch depicts St Gregory in the Forum at Rome. Asking the origin of some slave children, he was told they were Anglo-Saxons. Above are the famous words of his reply: 'Not Angles, but angels, if they were but Christians'.

In this chapel lie buried two great Catholic leaders of this country. Bishop Richard Challoner (1691–1781) lived during a period of great difficulty for the Catholic Church in England. Working in secret, he founded schools and charities for the poor, and ministered faithfully to the small Catholic population. Bishop Challoner narrowly escaped attack in the anti-Catholic Gordon Riots of 1780, but died soon afterwards.

Cardinal George Basil Hume (1923–1999) was a monk of Ampleforth Abbey, Yorkshire. In 1963 he was elected abbot, where his wisdom and holiness earned him great respect. Basil Hume was installed as ninth Archbishop of Westminster on 25 March 1976 and was created cardinal by Pope Paul VI. An outstanding leader of the Church, his humility, prayerfulness and foresight made him a popular figure well beyond the Catholic community. He was awarded the Order of Merit by Her Majesty the Queen in 1999 – a unique distinction for a Catholic prelate. His funeral in 1999 was attended by leaders of Church and State, as well as thousands of the faithful people whom he had served so devotedly.

ABOVE Pope St Gregory is traditionally represented with a dove, symbol of the Holy Spirit. St Augustine holds the icon of Christ he brought with him to England.

BELOW Above the tomb of Basil Hume hangs his cardinal's hat (*galero*), which traditionally remains until it falls.

St Patrick (AD 387–461) brought the Christian faith to the Irish people and is venerated as patron saint of Ireland. Famously, he used the shamrock to illustrate for them the doctrine of the Trinity, and, accordingly, the shamrock can be seen throughout the chapel: on the border of the rear wall, in mother-of-pearl behind the altar, in the wooden furniture – and even in the iron candlestand outside the chapel. Shamrocks are also carved into the white marble screen that separates the chapel from the main cathedral, accompanied by the oak leaves of St Brigid.

Green, the traditional colour of Ireland, is dominant in the chapel, with much of its marble originating from Cork and Connemara. Celtic designs, reflecting those of ancient Irish manuscripts, are inlaid on the floor and at the foot of the altar.

The snakes which curl around the altar recall the legend of St Patrick driving the snakes out of Ireland, a symbol of the triumph of good over evil.

Above the altar is a bronze gilt statue of St Patrick, designed in 1961 by Arthur Pollen in the style of an ancient Celtic carving. Nearby is a mosaic of St Patrick by Trevor Caley, erected in 1999 and blessed by the Archbishop of Tuam.

Around the chapel walls are the badges of Irish regiments that fought in the First World War (1914–1918). In a casket by the altar are inscribed the names of 50,000 Irish soldiers who died at that time. In 1996 the President of Ireland, Mary Robinson, prayed in the chapel and laid a wreath to the dead commemorated here; her visit was repeated by President Mary McAleese in 2001.

Outside the chapel, a mosaic by Boris Anrep commemorates St Oliver Plunkett, Archbishop of Armagh. St Oliver was the last person in England to die for the Catholic faith, and was executed at Tyburn in 1681.

ABOVE The details of the chapel portray Irish designs and themes associated with St Patrick.

BELOW The statue of St Patrick portrays him with his bishop's crozier, as first religious leader of the Irish people.

St Andrew is the patron saint of Scotland: many of the marbles in this chapel come from Scotland, and the thistle (the emblem of Scotland) can be seen on top of the chapel grille. Either side of the altar are depicted four Scottish saints – Ninian, Margaret, Bride and Columba – and the names of other saints of Scotland are carved around the walls.

The furniture of the chapel is especially fine. Superbly crafted in ebony and ivory, the stalls and kneelers are the work of Ernest Gimson, a leader in the Arts and Crafts movement.

The decoration of the chapel follows the tradition of Byzantine art, recalling the fact that St Andrew is also patron saint of Greece. The central lamp and the grille include representations of the ostrich egg, the Byzantine symbol of eternity. Above the arches are represented towns associated with St Andrew and his relics.

St Andrew's trade as a fisherman is recalled in the mosaic of the ceiling, designed to resemble fish scales, and by the floor, where a river is depicted meandering alongside fish and sea life.

BELOW The chapel was unveiled on the feast of St Andrew in 1915, when the Marquess of Bute served Mass for Cardinal Bourne.

ABOVE The 4th Marquess of Bute paid for the furnishings of this chapel, which reflect his Scottish nationality and interest in Byzantine studies.

CHAPEL OF ST PAUL

St Paul, together with St Peter, founded the Church at Rome. As a young man he was a ruthless persecutor of the Christian faith. The back wall of this chapel portrays the story of his conversion. Travelling from Jerusalem to Damascus, Paul is blinded, and is addressed by Christ: 'Get up, and go into the city, and you will be told what to do' (Acts 9:6). The ceiling of the chapel is decorated to represent a tent, recalling Paul's original profession as a tent-maker.

On the right of the chapel Paul is shown shipwrecked on Malta. The mosaic over the arch opposite represents the riddle of Samson (Judges 14:14): bees around the head of a lion represent sweetness coming forth from strength, a reference to Paul's good works following his former bitterness towards Christianity. Also depicted is a basket, recalling Paul's escape from Damascus when he was lowered over the wall (Acts 9:25).

Over the altar, Paul is shown with his traditional sword – a symbol both of his eloquence and of his death. The marble behind the altar comes from Athens, where Paul himself preached. Above, Christ is depicted with St Peter and St Paul, and the Latin inscription translates 'The Lord gives us the Law'.

The floor of the chapel is in the style of the Cosmati brothers, who worked in Italy in the twelfth and thirteenth centuries, and recalls the magnificent Cosmati pavement of Westminster Abbey.

OPPOSITE PAGE AND BELOW The mosaics, completed in 1963, are the work of Justin Vulliamy, pupil of Boris Anrep.

SOUTH TRANSEPT

The medieval alabaster statue of the Virgin and Child, under the thirteenth station, is a masterpiece from the celebrated Nottingham workshops, and survived the Reformation by being transported abroad. It is enshrined in the cathedral under the title *Our Lady of Westminster*, recalling the medieval shrine that once stood in Westminster Abbey. Two medieval wrought-iron candle-holders flank the image.

Nearby on the same pier is a bronze relief of St Thérèse of Liseux by Giacomo Manzù.

XIII. THE BODY OF JESUS IS TAKEN FR[OM] THE CROSS AND LAID IN MARY'S BOS[OM]

Its simplicity is characteristic of Manzù, who was a close friend of Pope John XXIII. Installed in 1958, this is the only work of the artist outside Italy.

To the right are the confessionals, where cathedral priests hear confessions for several hours each day. In the arch closest to the Lady Chapel, some of the earliest mosaics in the cathedral depict St Peter with the inscription, 'And he went out and wept bitterly' (Luke 22:62), and St Mary Magdalene with the words 'Her sins which were many have been forgiven' (Luke 7:47). Located near the confessionals, Peter and Mary Magdalene are fitting examples of penitence and forgiveness. Above the confessionals are bronze reliefs of St Vincent de Paul and St Benedict. Between them is a war memorial to the Royal Canadian Air Force, made from hundreds of flat-headed nails forming the Greek letter Chi-Rho, signifying the name of Christ.

ABOVE Nottingham alabasters were widely famous in the Middle Ages, and exported throughout Europe. The statue of Our Lady of Westminster provides a strong link with the medieval church.

CHAPEL OF THE BLESSED VIRGIN MARY

The Virgin Mary, mother of Jesus (known as 'Our Lady'), has a special place in the hearts of Catholics. It was here, on the Feast of the Annunciation in 1903, that the first Mass was celebrated in Westminster Cathedral.

The rich decoration of this chapel gives some vision of the completed cathedral. At the altar is an image of the Virgin and the child Jesus. Above, Jesus stands on the Cross – represented as the Tree of Life. From it gush fountains of water, while its branches produce vines, a refuge for the birds of the air.

To the left of the tree stands Mary, in front of the Tower of London and Tower Bridge. Next to her is Gabriel, archangel of the Annunciation, and a group of saints renowned for their devotion to the Virgin Mary. To the right of the tree is St Peter, in front of Westminster Cathedral.

The domed vault is marked with a wreath, containing portraits of the first four Cardinals of Westminster.

Just above the marble, a frieze depicts scenes from the life

BELOW The exquisite decoration of this chapel indicates the special place Mary enjoys in the hearts of Catholics.

OPPOSITE PAGE The chapel
of the Blessed Virgin
Mary, in its perfection
of mosaic and marble,
allows us to glimpse
the effect of the
completed cathedral.

of Mary, beginning with the
betrothal of her parents and
concluding with her death
(*Dormition*). Scenes above
recount the role of Mary in the life of the Church, including the
Promulgation of the Doctrine of the Immaculate Conception by
Pope Pius IX in 1854, and the appearance of Mary to St Bernadette
at Lourdes.

ABOVE Across the chapel,
the imposing decoration
of the sanctuary is
revealed.

The window recesses bear portraits of early women martyrs:
St Lucy, St Agatha, St Justine, St Cecilia and St Catherine, while
in the four alcoves are represented prophets who foretold the coming
of the Messiah: Daniel, Ezekiel, Jeremiah, Isaiah.

The crypt is dedicated to St Peter. A vigorous mosaic by Gilbert Pownall represents the saint enthroned and holding the keys of authority entrusted to him by Christ (Matt 16:19). To the left, Peter tries to walk towards the Lord over the water, and on the right he receives the keys from Jesus.

On the opposite side of the crypt, set into the floor by the curved wall, is the tomb of Cardinal Griffin, sixth Archbishop of Westminster (1943–1956). Nearby stands the large sarcophagus of Cardinal Godfrey, seventh Archbishop of Westminster (1956–1963). Their cardinal's hats hang above their graves.

In the corner is the tomb of the only lay person to be buried in the cathedral. Count Alexander Benckendorff was the last ambassador from tsarist Russia to the Court of St James. At his death in 1917, it proved impossible to return his body to Russia, and so he was buried at Westminster Cathedral beneath a slab inscribed in Russian and Latin by Eric Gill.

Through the iron gates lies the Chapel of St Edmund of Canterbury (1175–1240), a patron of Westminster Diocese. Here, directly under the high altar of the cathedral, are buried the first two Archbishops of

BELOW The dedication of the crypt to St Peter recalls the tomb of the saint beneath the high altar of St Peter's in Rome.

OPPOSITE PAGE The crypt is not normally open to the public, but is used for special groups and school Masses.

Westminster, Cardinal Wiseman (1850–1865) and Cardinal Manning (1865–1892). Originally interred in St Mary's Catholic cemetery in Kensal Green, they were removed to Westminster in 1907. Nearby, the altar of St Edmund preserves his relics, beneath a fine mosaic representing the saint blessing London.

The sanctuary is the focus of the Cathedral, where Mass, the principal act of worship for Catholics, takes place. Bentley intended all the perspective lines of the Cathedral to converge at this point – in particular upon the altar where Mass is celebrated. The high altar itself is a single block of unpolished Cornish granite, three and a half metres long and weighing 12.2 tonnes. Upon the altar is positioned a two-metre high crucifix, bearing alpha and omega pendants – the first and last letters of the Greek alphabet, symbolising the universality of Christ's power. On each side stand six great candlesticks; a seventh is added behind the crucifix when the Cardinal Archbishop celebrates Mass. Before the altar, the floor of the sanctuary is carpeted in exquisite marble designs, sadly invisible to all but the clergy in the sanctuary.

Above the altar towers the great stone canopy, or *baldacchino* (from an Arabic word describing a tent), recalling the tent erected over the Holy of Holies in the Old Testament. The *baldacchino* was always intended by Bentley to be the crowning glory of his cathedral, and he was especially influenced by the church of Sant' Ambrogio in Milan. Its eight magnificent columns are of yellow Verona marble, each four and a half metres high. The *baldacchino* was unveiled at Christmas Midnight Mass in 1906.

To the left is the throne of the Archbishop of Westminster; its proper Latin name, *cathedra,* is the origin of the word 'cathedral'. Our *cathedra* at Westminster Cathedral is a smaller copy of that in the basilica of St John Lateran in Rome – the Pope's own cathedral and the seat of his authority as Bishop of Rome. In every cathedral, the authority of its bishop is most clearly symbolised when he presides from the throne and preaches to the faithful. The Westminster *cathedra* was a gift to Cardinal Vaughan from the Catholic bishops of England and Wales in 1900.

To the sides, the fine choir stalls of Austrian oak provide seating for the cathedral canons, chaplains and altar servers. The benches in the front row bear the names of Old Testament prophets, in their Latin version, culminating in Christ.

OPPOSITE PAGE AND RIGHT The high altar provides the visual and spiritual focus of the cathedral. Here Mass is celebrated daily.

The back wall of the sanctuary is pierced by four arched openings, which give light to the crypt beneath. Above is raised the semicircular domed apse, from where the choir sings (unlike in other cathedrals, the choir at Westminster is not seen by the congregation during services, so that their music provides a disembodied and heavenly backdrop to the liturgy). In the centre of the apse, a tablet of white Carrara marble bears an image of Christ holding a chalice of his blood – a further reference to the cathedral's dedication, and serving to screen the Master of Music as he conducts the choir.

Suspended high above the sanctuary is the great rood (cross) of painted and gilt wood, recalling the dedication of Westminster Cathedral: the Most Precious Blood of our Lord Jesus Christ. The cross is ten metres high and weighs two tonnes, and the figure of Christ is six metres tall. The traditional emblems of the four evangelists occupy the extremities of the arms: a lion represents St Mark, a bull St Luke, an eagle St John, and a man St Matthew.

On the reverse side of the cross is the figure of Mary as Our Lady of Sorrows, a sword piercing her heart in fulfilment of Simeon's prophecy. Surrounded by texts from the Lenten hymn *Stabat Mater*, she stands at the head of the congregation, as the first of humanity to be redeemed by Christ's sacrifice.

Partially concealed by the great rood is a 1934 mosaic by Gilbert Pownall, depicting Christ enthroned in majesty in the heavens above a globe of the world and holding a chalice of his Precious Blood. He is surrounded by the familiar emblems of the evangelists, and contemplated by the twelve apostles in glory. The blue background to the scene is composed of hundreds of faces of the heavenly angels. An inscription surrounds the arch, taken from the Latin hymn *Te Deum*, which reads:

OPPOSITE PAGE The view from the apse provides a panorama of the cathedral. On the reverse of the great rood, Mary seems to lead the congregation in worship.

JUDEX CREDERIS ESSE VENTURUS. TE ERGO
QUAESUMUS, TUIS FAMULIS SUBVENI, QUOS
PRETIOSO SANGUINE REDEMISTI
(We believe you are the judge who is to come.
Therefore we beseech you, come to the aid of
your servants whom you have redeemed by your
precious blood).

Gilbert Pownall completed this work
immediately after his successful decoration in
the Lady Chapel. In this case, however, the
results were heavily criticised for the weak
treatment of a complex subject. Pownall had
already begun to decorate the domed apse,
but under relentless pressure from the artistic
establishment, which included letters in
The Times newspaper, Cardinal Bourne had the
new mosaics removed – apart from the floral
arch at the edge.

OPPOSITE PAGE
The *cathedra* of the
Archbishop is the
visual symbol of his
authority in the
diocese of
Westminster.

At the foot of the sanctuary steps is a Latin
inscription commemorating the visit of Pope
John Paul II to Westminster Cathedral in 1982 –
the only visit ever by a reigning Pope to Britain. The plaque is the
gift of the Friends of Westminster Cathedral, and reads:

ECCE VESTIGIA SUMMI PASTORIS
IOANNIS PAULI II
QUI IN ANGLIA PEREGRINATOR
PRIMAM MISSAM HIC CELELBRAVIT
DIE 28 MAII 1982
IN OMNIBUS GLORIFICETUR DEUS
(Behold the footsteps of the Supreme Shepherd John Paul II,
who as pilgrim to England celebrated his first Mass here
on 28 May 1982. May God be glorified in all things.)

LEFT The great
national and diocesan
ceremonies of the
Catholic Church in
England and Wales are
accompanied by the
music of the celebrated
Westminster Cathedral
Choir.

CHAPEL OF THE BLESSED SACRAMENT

In the chapel of the Blessed Sacrament, the Eucharist is reserved in the form of consecrated bread within the veiled tabernacle on the altar, to provide communion for the sick, and for private devotion. This is one of the most sacred places in the cathedral: a place of quiet prayer, where the sanctuary lamps burn constantly before the presence of the Lord.

The mosaics of this chapel, executed by the Russian artist Boris Anrep in 1962, portray images from the Old and New Testaments symbolising the Eucharist. Anrep had already decorated many public buildings in London, including the National Gallery and the Bank of England, when the cathedral authorities approached him with the chapel commission. Instead of the usual gold, Anrep employed pastel hues, predominantly pink. Drawing upon the orthodox traditions of his native Russia, his depiction of biblical figures is iconic and formal, as may be seen in the archangels Michael and Gabriel who stand guard at the entrance to the chapel. Between them a three-domed church symbolises the Trinity, setting the Eucharist within the greater mystery of the Godhead. The nave of the chapel contains scenes from the Old Testament that are traditionally held to prefigure the Eucharist; among them are the sacrifices of Abraham, Noah, Abel and Melchizedek. On the wall behind the entrance, Anrep has depicted the hospitality of Abraham, receiving three heavenly visitors – interpreted as an image of the Trinity.

BELOW The screen of the Blessed Sacrament Chapel, in enamel and bronze, took over three years to create.
BELOW RIGHT Hexagonal silver lamps, set with precious stones, always burn before the reserved Sacrament.

OPPOSITE PAGE The pelican is an ancient image of piety; it was believed she fed her children from her pierced breast. The bird came to symbolise Christ's sacrifice.

In the domed apse, the figure of Christ is flanked by symbols of the Father and the Holy Spirit. Below is a jewelled cross, sign of Christ's glorious victory, before which stands St Peter's Basilica, founded upon the rock from which flow the four rivers of paradise. On either side are depicted the key events of our salvation: the Resurrection and the liberation of the souls in Hell. At the edges of the apse are two scenes from the New Testament that anticipate the Eucharist: the marriage at Cana and Christ's feeding of the multitude.

Just before the entrance to the chapel, a small 'aviary' is formed from the mosaic representations of the peacock (symbol of eternity) and the phoenix (symbol of the Resurrection), and a bronze pelican atop the grille. In the Middle Ages it was widely believed that the pelican fed her young by piercing her own breast, and so the bird became a symbol of the sacrifice of Christ.

BELOW The three young men in the furnace, from the Book of Daniel, are a reference to the Trinity. The grapes symbolise the Eucharist.

CHAPEL OF THE SACRED HEART AND ST MICHAEL

This tiny gem of a chapel is often overlooked, but is one of the most prayerful and beautiful spots in the cathedral. Its rich mosaic ceiling is patterned on the ancient monuments of Rome and Ravenna, which rejected pictorial representation in favour of sumptuous carpet-like design. The predominance of red mosaic recalls the dedication of the cathedral to the Most Precious Blood, as does the depiction on the west wall of the head of Christ in his Passion. This image is based upon the work of Christian Symons – responsible for the great rood above the high altar.

The authentic Byzantine feel of the chapel extends even to light fittings. They are modelled on those in Haghia Sophia, the great basilica of Constantinople, and reconstructed from the descriptions of a sixth-century author.

On the altar is a large statue of the Sacred Heart, a popular devotional image in Catholicism. Christ here is shown bestowing love from his wounded heart – a heart which, for love of us, he permitted to be pierced by our sins. This statue was given to the cathedral by the nuns of the Order of the Sacred Heart and by pupils from their schools. On the front of the altar is depicted the archangel Michael slaying a dragon – which represents Satan and all the enemies of Christ and his Church.

RIGHT The jewel-like chapel of the Sacred Heart is a place of quiet prayer and devotion.

CHAPEL OF ᔆᵀ THOMAS OF CANTERBURY

This small chapel was founded as a chantry chapel – that is, a chapel where Mass would be offered for the soul of the cathedral's founder, Cardinal Vaughan. The screen before the chapel bears the Cardinal's initials and coat of arms. The Cardinal himself lies beneath a fine effigy, having been buried originally at Mill Hill – the missionary institute in north London that is his other great foundation.

The mosaics, designed by Christopher Hobbs, represent the chapel's dedication to St Thomas of Canterbury – Thomas à Becket – who was murdered in Canterbury Cathedral in 1170. The depiction of St Thomas, like the decoration throughout the chapel, carefully recalls the style of English Romanesque art ontemporary with the martyr.

RIGHT Cardinal Vaughan's funeral was the first major ceremony to take place in Westminster Cathedral.

St Joseph, the carpenter, was the husband of Mary, mother of Jesus. He is depicted above the altar in the triptych bearing the tools of the carpenter's trade. The large mosaic of the Holy Family in the apse, by Christopher Hobbs, was completed in June 2003.

The marble work in this chapel is particularly fine, with a column of exquisite *cipollino* (onion skin) marble at the centre. The capital of the column shows a basket of doves, recalling the doves presented by Mary and Joseph at the Temple.

In the centre of the pavement are four symbols of Christ: the lamb, the peacock (symbol of eternity), the fish, and the Chi-Rho (made from the first two letters of Christ's name in Greek).

Buried in the chapel is Cardinal Hinsley, fifth Archbishop of Westminster, who died in 1943. Cardinal Hinsley became famous for his wartime radio chats and stirring encouragement. His red cardinal's hat hangs above his tomb, and is allowed to decay as a reminder of the mortality common to all.

Niches outside the chapel represent St Nicholas, in his less common role as protector of seafarers, and St Christopher, patron of travellers by land and sea.

OPPOSITE PAGE The prayers for St Joseph's feast day state: 'With a husband's love he cherished Mary, the virgin Mother of God. With fatherly care he watched over Jesus, conceived by the power of the Holy Spirit'.
ABOVE Byzantine forms and imagery have been skilfully adapted in this chapel.

St George was a Roman solider, put to death for his Christian faith about AD 320. His cult was brought to England by the Crusaders, and King Edward III made him patron of England in the fourteenth century. This chapel is dedicated to England, those who have witnessed to their Catholic faith in our land, and those who have died in the world wars. Panels list servicemen who gave their lives in battle, and who are prayed for in the cathedral.

In the centre of the floor is a rose, symbol of England, inlaid with lapis lazuli and mother-of-pearl; the rose motif is continued behind the altar and around the walls. Either side of the altar the red cross of St George is displayed on marble shields.

On the facing wall is a carving by Lindsey Clark of St George, patron of England. Above the altar is the last carving of Eric Gill. It portrays Christ on the cross, not as victim, but gloriously triumphant over death; to his left stands St Thomas More, Lord Chancellor of England, and to his right St John Fisher, Bishop of Rochester. Both men were executed in 1535 for their refusal to deny the supremacy of the Pope under King Henry VIII.

ABOVE The image of St Alban reflects the artist's research into Egyptian portraits contemporary with the saint.
BELOW The imagery of this chapel carefully proclaims its dedication to England.

In a shrine by the grille lies the body of St John Southworth, martyred in 1654 at Tyburn (now Marble Arch) for his Catholic faith. During his life, St John ministered to the poor in the area near where the cathedral now stands. His remains were brought to the cathedral in 1930.

The chair and kneeler in the chapel were made for the visit of Queen Elizabeth II in 1995 – the first time since the Reformation that a reigning monarch has attended a Roman Catholic service.

At the entrance to the chapel is a mosaic of

ABOVE The face of St John Southworth is covered by a silver mask. He lies close to the area in which he once ministered.
BELOW Military associations are present in the shield of St George, and the mosaic donated by the Royal Army Medical Corps.

ABOVE Behind the altar, white roses in mother-of-pearl set in red marble continue the chapel's English theme.

Christ the Divine Healer, erected in 1952 in memory of the Royal Army Medical Corps.

Outside the chapel, a mosaic portrays St Alban, the first to shed his blood for the Christian faith in England. Alban was a Roman soldier who sheltered, and then changed places with, a priest. When arrested, refusing to sacrifice to the Roman gods, he was martyred. The mosaic, by Christopher Hobbs, was unveiled in June 2001.

OPPOSITE PAGE At the throne of Christ, Mary and Joseph intercede for the Holy Souls. The donors of the panel may just be glimpsed in the corners.

The Holy Souls are the dead who, according to Catholic belief, wait in Purgatory for final purification before entering Heaven, helped by the prayers of the living.

The decoration of this chapel, with its ghostly silver vault and sombre black marble, was designed by the cathedral architect, John Francis Bentley, and executed by Christian Symons.

Images in this chapel show the 'old' Adam by the forbidden tree, contrasted with the 'new' Adam – the risen Christ. On the west wall is a powerful image of Purgatory from the Book of Daniel: Shadrach, Meshach and Abednego, cast into the burning fiery furnace, are protected by the Son of Man.

Above the altar, a mosaic depicts the archangel Raphael escorting souls through the cleansing flames, while below, Christ in judgement displays his wounds – another reference to the dedication of the cathedral.

Two panels either side of the entrance recall the first performance here of the *Dream of Gerontius*, Elgar's setting of Cardinal Newman's poem, in 1903. They were designed by Tom Phillips, RA, in 2003.

ABOVE AND LEFT The sombre tones of this chapel perhaps reflect a Victorian fascination with the Final Judgement.

With its multiple roles as national shrine, mother church of
Westminster Diocese and parish church in a busy city, Westminster
Cathedral will always be more than a monument or an historic
building. It is a house of God that is lived in and – more importantly –
prayed in. At all hours, whether at a great ceremony, a quiet Mass,
or during a peaceful afternoon, the cathedral is home to all who wish
to pray, reflect, and find peace.

Westminster Cathedral provides a busy schedule of services for the
many faithful who throng to its doors. Each weekday six Masses are
celebrated, with seven on a Sunday. Lauds and Vespers are sung at
the beginning and end of each day, and confessions are heard all day,
every day.

LEFT AND BELOW Solemn
Mass, celebrated by the
clergy of the cathedral
and accompanied by the
choir, is a powerful
spiritual experience.

ABOVE The choristers at Westminster live in the nearby Choir School, and rehearse for many hours each day.

During Holy Week each year, just before Easter, the cardinal presides at Mass with his auxiliary bishops, priests, deacons and faithful. This 'Chrism Mass' (where the sacred oil, or chrism, is blessed) most perfectly represents the role of the cathedral as the mother church of Westminster Diocese, where the faithful are gathered in unity and worship around their bishop. In addition, the cathedral hosts the great ceremonies of the Church's year – as at Christmas and Easter – and the major feasts, usually celebrated by the cardinal. Other significant events naturally find a home here; organizations and individuals are commemorated in special services, while baptisms, weddings and funerals are regularly celebrated at the cathedral altars. All this requires a dedicated team of cathedral chaplains, presided over by the Administrator and supported by a large team of staff and volunteers.

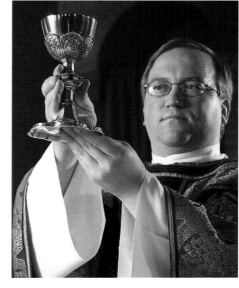

Each day solemn Mass is sung by the celebrated choir of Westminster Cathedral, a fact unique among the cathedrals of the world.

The choir at Westminster was founded by Cardinal Vaughan in 1902, and under the inspired leadership of its first Master of Music, Sir Richard Terry, rapidly established itself as one of the foremost choirs in the land. Terry's researches into sixteenth-century polyphony uncovered a neglected treasury of masterpieces, for which the Westminster Cathedral Choir became famous. Singular, also, is its sound – often, but misleadingly, called 'continental', but certainly unlike any other cathedral choir in the country and particularly suited to the Latin polyphony which is its staple repertoire.

Historical monument, artistic masterpiece, famous landmark; while it is all these things, Westminster Cathedral is, and will remain, above all a house of prayer, where tourist and pilgrim alike may experience God, and find refreshment for their souls.

ABOVE The soaring architecture of Bentley's masterpiece forms a majestic backdrop to the celebration of the liturgy.

BELOW Solemn Mass is celebrated every day in the cathedral, to the high standards desired by Cardinal Vaughan.

CONTACTS AND SERVICES

TIMES OF SERVICES

Sunday

8.00 am	Mass
9.00 am	Mass
10.00 am	Morning Prayer
10.30 am	**Solemn Mass** (*sung*)
12.00 noon	Mass
3.30 pm	**Solemn Vespers and Benediction** (*sung*)
5.30 pm	Mass
7.00 pm	Mass

Monday–Friday

7.00 am	Mass
7.40 am	Morning Prayer
8.00 am	Mass
10.30 am	Mass (*Latin*)
12.30 pm	Mass
1.05 pm	Mass
5.00 pm	**Vespers** (*sung*)
5.30 pm	**Solemn Mass** (*sung*)

Saturday

8.00 am	Mass
9.00 am	Mass
10.00 am	Morning Prayer
10.30 am	**Solemn Mass** (*sung*)
12.30 pm	Mass
5.30 pm	Evening Prayer
6.00 pm	Mass (First of Sunday)

Public Holidays

8.00 am	Mass
10.00 am	Morning Prayer
10.30 am	Mass
12.30 pm	Mass

PUBLIC SERVICES

The cathedral opens shortly before the first Mass of the day; doors close at 7.00 pm, Monday to Saturday, with occasional exceptions. On Sunday evenings, the cathedral closes after the 7.00 pm Mass. On public and bank holidays the cathedral closes at 5.30 pm in the afternoon (no Evening Prayer).

CONTACT DETAILS

Westminster Cathedral

42 Francis Street
London
SW1P 1QW
United Kingdom
Telephone: 020 7798 9055
Fax: 020 7798 9090
Website: www.westminstercathedral.org.uk
Registered Charity Number 233699

INFORMATION DESK

The information desk is located at the back of the nave in the cathedral and is open daily from 10.00 am to 5.00 pm.

ISBN 0-7117-4149-2
© Jarrold Publishing and Westminster Cathedral. 2005
All rights reserved. No part of this publication may be reproduced, stored in a retrieval system or transmitted in any form or by any means, electronic, mechanical, photocopying or otherwise, without the prior permission in writing of the publisher.
Designed and produced by Jarrold Publishing
Text by Monsignor Mark Langham
Photography by Peter Smith of Newbery Smith Photography, except p39 (centre) by Neil Jinkerson of Jarrold Publishing
Project Manager: Malcolm Crampton
Design: Kaarin Wall
Printed in Great Britain. Jarrold Publishing 1/05
www.jarrold-publishing.co.uk